JOEL
the Amazing Fisher of Men

Illustrated by:
Maryna Kovinka

Gloria
Harrison

Joel: The Amazing Fisher of Men

ISBN 978-1-949185-00-3 (Hardcover Ed)
ISBN 978-1-949185-01-0 (Paperback Ed)
Cataloging-in-Publication date on file with the publisher.

Published by Gloria M. Harrison
Dover, DE 19903

Illustrated by: Maryna Kovinka
Design and production: Gloria M. Harrison

Printed in the United States of America
10 9 8 7 6 5 4 3 2 1

It was Sunday morning, the last day before Joel's vacation. Mom said he was going to Sunday school.

4

"Joel, it's getting late," said Mom.
"I'll be right there," replied Joel.

5

When Joel got to Church, he didn't see his friends,
Tyler and Mac. Ms. Sharpe said they had left for
vacation.
Joel was hoping they would be in class today. At least
he won't get into any trouble with Ms. Sharpe today.

6

"Good morning. Our lesson today is about four amazing fishermen," said Ms. Sharpe. Some of the girls held their nose. "Fishermen!" Joel said while almost falling out his seat.

7

"I will be spending my summer with my uncle. He loves to fish and is going to teach me how to," said Joel.

"That's great Joel! These amazing fishermen loved to fish too.

One day, while they were fishing, Jesus walked by and said, follow Me and I will make you fishers of men. Do you know what happened next?" asked Ms. Sharpe.

The class was so excited. "They stopped fishing and
followed Jesus!" they shouted.
Ms. Sharpe laughed,
"Yes, these amazing fishermen stopped fishing and
followed Jesus to become fishers of men."
Joel wondered what it meant to become fisher of men.

"The disciples followed Jesus for a long time. When He died they were sad. Even though they saw Jesus after He had risen, they still decided to catch fish again. They fished all night and caught nothing," said Ms. Sharpe.
"Did Jesus make them disciples because they didn't do well with fishing?" Joel asked.

"No Joel. They were great fishermen," replied Ms. Sharpe.
"Now that morning, a man watched them clean their empty nets and told them to cast them out. They did not know it was Jesus, but they did what He said. They caught the biggest catch ever and needed a second boat. Soon they realized it was Jesus and they followed him."

Joel stared at Ms. Sharpe and imagined fishing for men.
He wondered how will they catch men.
Joel was puzzled. Men on a hook was too weird, but fish on a hook was just right.

He knew he could be a good fisherman, but he didn't know if he could be a fisher of men. Joel thought about the four fishermen and how they listened to Jesus. He realized he needed to listen to Uncle Bill if he wanted to become a fisherman.

"I will continue the lesson next week," Ms. Sharpe replied.

Joel would be on vacation next week, but he would ask all about it when he returned.

Joel couldn't stop thinking about being a fisher of men
and what it meant.
After dinner, he decided to practice catching fish until
it was time for bed.

Joel was so excited, he tossed and turned all night. He had a strange dream about people in a river jumping in and out of the water. They were crying. "Joel! Joel! Help us! We want to be caught! Please catch us!" "I want to catch you, but I can't! I don't know how to fish yet!" he replied.

Joel woke up thinking about the dream. He wondered if Peter, Andrew, James, and John had a dream like his.

16

Joel believed that if he was going to learn to catch
people, he had better learn to catch fish first.
"Sandy girl, we're going to have a great time!"

17

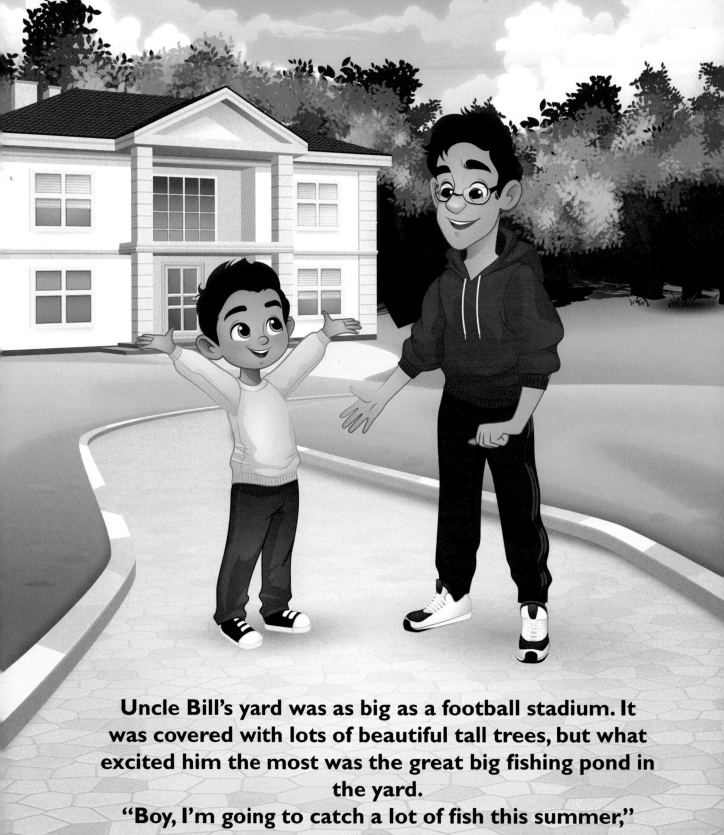

Uncle Bill's yard was as big as a football stadium. It was covered with lots of beautiful tall trees, but what excited him the most was the great big fishing pond in the yard.

"Boy, I'm going to catch a lot of fish this summer," said Joel.

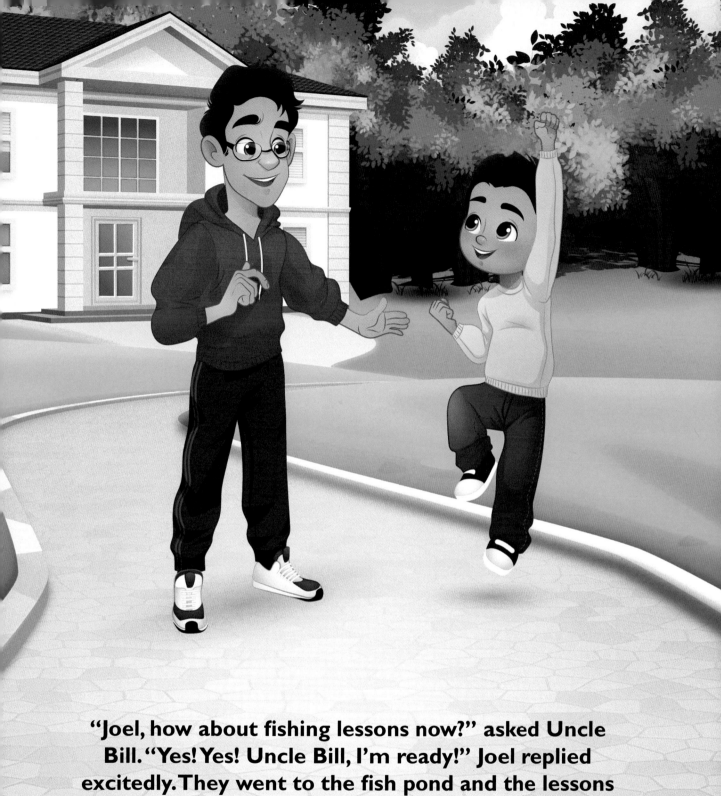

"Joel, how about fishing lessons now?" asked Uncle Bill. "Yes! Yes! Uncle Bill, I'm ready!" Joel replied excitedly. They went to the fish pond and the lessons began.

Joel learned how to get his bait, put it on the hook, and
catch the fish. He was so excited he couldn't sit still.
"Joel, settle down or you will scare the fish away," said
Uncle Bill.
"Okay Uncle Bill," Joel replied as he settled down.

Suddenly, Joel felt a tug on his pole, so he tugged back.
Joel felt like he was catching the biggest fish in the
pond. What a great vacation this will be! He pulled
so hard that he got wrapped in the pole line and fell
landing face to face with a tiny fish.

21

After a week, Uncle Bill said Joel was ready to become a fisherman! Joel placed the bait on the hook and placed his line in the water. This was his first step: to becoming a fisherman. Next step: to become a fisher of men!

Joel felt the tug on his line! He knew this was a big
one! He was so excited he didn't see Sandy heading
towards him! She jumped into the pond and Joel
dropped his pole.

23

"I lost my fish! How can I be a fisherman with Sandy around?" said Joel.
"It's okay Joel. We still have plenty of time to catch fish together," Uncle Bill said.
"I've only caught one fish all summer. Well, the fish caught me. How can I be a fisher of men if I can't catch real fish?" Joel asked.
Uncle Bill was puzzled.

"Fisher of men?" Uncle Bill questioned.
Joel told Uncle Bill his Sunday School lesson about
the amazing fishermen and his dream about people
looking like fish and asking him to catch them.

Joel continued, "I want to be a fisherman just like the disciples. Jesus told them they would be fishers of men, but they were amazing fishers of fish first. I just know I must catch people. But how can I catch people if I can't catch fish?"

"I thought fishing was fun but when you can't catch the fish it's frustrating. Maybe catching people could be easier. At least you could see them better. Only, the disciples seemed to be good at both," said Joel.

"Fishing was all the disciples knew how to do. When they followed Jesus, they stopped fishing. When Jesus went to the cross, they lost all hope," Uncle Bill replied. "Even though He rose again, and they saw Him, they still went fishing for fish after 3 years."
"Three years! Maybe they really did forget how to fish!" Joel blurted out.

Early the next morning, Joel and Uncle Bill went back to fishing. "Uncle Bill, why did they go back to fishing? Did they miss it?" Joel asked.

"No, they felt lost and didn't know what to do when Jesus went to the cross. It took them seeing Him three times after He had risen before they remembered they were called to be fishers of men."

Uncle Bill continued, "Jesus called them to care for
people the way He cared for them; to teach them how
to love like God and to follow Him.
"Like they followed Jesus, Uncle Bill?" Joel added with
excitement.
"Yes, remember what Jesus said to Peter, if you love
Me feed My lambs and My sheep. Tend to My people
and teach them My purpose for them," said Uncle Bill.

"Peter was a great fisher of men once he listened to Jesus," Joel said.
"Jesus called Peter to teach His people God's word. Your Sunday School teacher is a fisher of men because she teaches you God's word," said Uncle Bill.
"I think I got it Uncle Bill, everybody can be fishers of men if they follow Jesus!"

"So that means, I am a fisher of men because I follow Jesus and tell people how to follow Him!" Joel shouted. "I told my friends Tyler and Mac about how Jesus loves them and now they follow Him too!"
"See Joel, you are already a fisher of men!" replied Uncle Bill.
Joel smiled, "I am! I am already an amazing fisher of men for God!"

"Uncle Bill! I got a fish and I think it's a big one!" said Joel as he struggled to hold on to his pole.

Precious Memories!

"Now, I am like the disciples, Uncle Bill!
I am a fisher of fish and an amazing fisher of men for
God!"

34

Made in the USA
Columbia, SC
24 March 2020

89882612R00020